Produced by AA Publishing

Captions by Richard Cavendish

Filmset by Wyvern Typesetting Ltd, Bristol
Origination by Scantrans Pte Ltd, Singapore
Printed and bound by New Interlitho SpA, Italy

The contents of this publication are believed correct
at the time of printing. Nevertheless, the publishers
cannot accept responsibility for errors or omissions,
or for changes in details given.

A CIP catalogue record for this book is available
from the British Library.

Published by The Automobile Association, Fanum
House, Basing View, Basingstoke, Hampshire
RG21 2EA.

ISBN 0 7495 0150 2

Front cover: Top – *Horse Guards Parade*
Main – *Tower Bridge and fireworks*
Back cover: *Burlington Arcade entrance with Penhaligon van drawn up*
Title page (opposite): *Parliament Square*

visions·of
LONDON

Visions of London takes a look at one of the world's most renowned capitals. The photographs reveal a city full of tradition and history, and show its more familiar sights – the hustle and bustle of busy shops and market streets, excitement in its famous thoroughfares, the splendour of its architecture, as well as serene moments in parks and gardens.

Left *Tower Bridge from upstream, with the cruiser HMS* Belfast *moored on the left. The bridge's Gothic towers support the two ponderous 1000-ton leaves of the drawbridge, about 30ft (9m) above high water, which rise to let ships through. In 1952 a bus was caught on the drawbridge as it started to rise and jumped several feet across the widening gap to the other side.*

Left *London's best-known bridge is a symbol of the city for many visitors. Tower Bridge was opened in 1894 by the Prince of Wales (the future King Edward VII). The Tower of London and the high-rise City office blocks can be seen behind.*

Above *David Wynne's spectacular 1973 bronze* Girl with a Dolphin, *with Tower Bridge behind. The bridge has been powered by electricity since 1976, but the original steam machinery for raising the drawbridge can still be seen, and there are wonderful views from the high crosswalks.*

Right *London's pubs, of every date and style from the 16th century on, are a vital ingredient of the city's character. The Black Friar, in Queen Victoria Street near Blackfriars Bridge, is the capital's only completely Art Nouveau public house, with delightful 1900s murals of jolly friars inside.*

Right *The Widow's Son in Bow is close to the river. It was built in 1848 and every year a fresh hot cross bun is added to the collection hanging from the ceiling. They were originally baked, Easter after Easter, by a widow for her son, who was missing at sea and never returned.*

Left *The oldest riverside public house in London, the low-beamed Prospect of Whitby in Wapping, was originally built in 1520. Samuel Pepys and Judge Jeffreys knew it well, and later so did Charles Dickens and the painters Turner and Whistler.*

Left *The Golden Lion is a handsome Victorian hostelry in King Street, St James's. The street was laid out in the 17th century and a tavern of this name has stood on the site since at least 1762.*

Left *Powerful Shire horses with their massive hooves and bulky harness, hauling drays laden with beer barrels, were once a familiar sight on London's streets. Young's Brewery in Wandsworth still uses them to make deliveries, here to the imposing 18th-century Old Sergeant Inn in Garratt Lane.*

Below *A pause for refreshment at the Cross Keys public house in Endell Street, in the Covent Garden area. It was built in 1854, when this street was driven through the district's slums. The crossed keys held by the cherubs are those of St Peter, who traditionally holds the keys of heaven and hell.*

London

Left *The dome of St Paul's Cathedral rises in Baroque majesty through the evening sky. Sir Christopher Wren's masterpiece replaced Old St Paul's, which was destroyed in the Great Fire of London in 1666. The architect was buried inside in 1723, with the Latin epitaph:* Si monumentum requiris, circumspice – *'If you seek his monument, look around you'.*

Left *At the far end of the choir the high altar is shielded by a pillared marble canopy, which leads the eye up to the gilded mosaics of the vaulted ceiling, completed in 1912. The choir stalls and the organ case in dark oak were the work of Wren's contemporary, the master craftsman Grinling Gibbons.*

Left *Looking up Ludgate Hill to the west end of the cathedral. The splendid classical portico is flanked by twin towers, and behind them rises the vast dome, itself topped by a lantern and a cross, 365ft (111m) above street level.*

London

Right *London is rich in churches of every size, style and level of churchmanship. St Martin-in-the-Fields, on the corner of Trafalgar Square, has long been known for its work with the homeless. The elegant portico and steeple date from the 1720s, when the church was rebuilt by James Gibbs.*

Right *Rose window in St Katharine Cree in the City, in Leadenhall Street, which was rebuilt in the 17th century. The shape of the window recalls the wheel on which St Katharine was martyred.*

14

Left *Tomb of John Gower, the 14th-century poet and friend of Chaucer, in Southwark Cathedral. His rose-chapleted head rests on three of his books. The cathedral, formerly the parish church of St Mary Overie (meaning 'across the water' or possibly 'of the ferry') is considered London's finest medieval church after Westminster Abbey.*

Left *The imposing Oratory in Brompton Road, built on the model of a Renaissance church in Rome and completed in 1884, was the principal Roman Catholic church in London in the 19th century.*

Following spread *Every sovereign of England crowned since 1066 has been crowned in Westminster Abbey, where many of the nation's great men and women are buried or commemorated. The church has been rebuilt and restored from the 13th century on, in the main in the same Gothic style. The nave is the highest of its period in the country, at 102ft (31m).*

15

Left *Pensioners on parade at the Royal Hospital in Chelsea, in their 18th-century uniforms with three-cornered hats. Some 400 old soldiers, most of them over 65, live at this home for army veterans, which was founded by Charles II.*

Left *Sir Christopher Wren was the architect of the Royal Hospital's handsome building in brick and stone, and King Charles laid the foundation stone in 1682. The Chelsea Flower Show is held in May every year in the extensive grounds, which run down towards the river.*

Above *A small museum covers the life and history of the Royal Hospital. The pensioners' everyday uniforms are smart in scarlet and black.*

Below *Central London is well supplied with public parks, which were originally royal pleasure grounds. The largest of them is Hyde Park, seen here with sculpture by Henry Moore. It was Henry VIII's hunting chase and deer were still hunted here in the 1760s.*

Right *A bird in the hand . . . a peaceful scene in Green Park, between Piccadilly and Buckingham Palace, which was once a notorious spot for duels. Charles II liked to picnic here and had the area laid out as a park in 1667.*

Left *A band concert in St James's Park, the oldest and perhaps the most attractive of them all. Henry VIII had a bowling alley and a deer park here, James I laid out formal gardens and Charles II redesigned it and liked to walk here with his spaniels and feed the birds.*

London

22

♔ ♔ ♔ ♔

Opposite page and top left
*Further out from town,
Londoners can enjoy the
rarities at the Royal Botanic
Gardens beside the Thames at
Kew, originally laid out for
George III and his mother, and
later landscaped by
Capability Brown. In the
soaring glasshouses palm
trees and tropical plants
flourish, however wintry the
weather outside.*

Bottom left *Other, less
spectacular glasshouses at
Kew nourish cacti and ferns,
orchids, water lilies and
plants which feed on insects.
Kew Gardens is a scientific
establishment for the study of
plants as well as an enjoyable
public garden.*

23

Following spread *An 18th-
century Chinese guardian lion
looks across the lake to the
superb glass-and-iron Palm
House of 1844–1848,
designed by Decimus Burton,
with Richard Taylor as
engineer. Ranged in front of it
stand the stern heraldic
figures of 'the Queen's
beasts', animals from the
royal coats of arms.*

Below London's variety of shops is encyclopedic and exhaustive, selling everything from angling equipment and answering machines to yarn and zip fasteners. The English reverence for tradition and for traditional costume supports unusual specialist shops like this one in Chancery Lane. Near the Law Courts and the Temple, it makes wigs and robes for the legal profession.

26

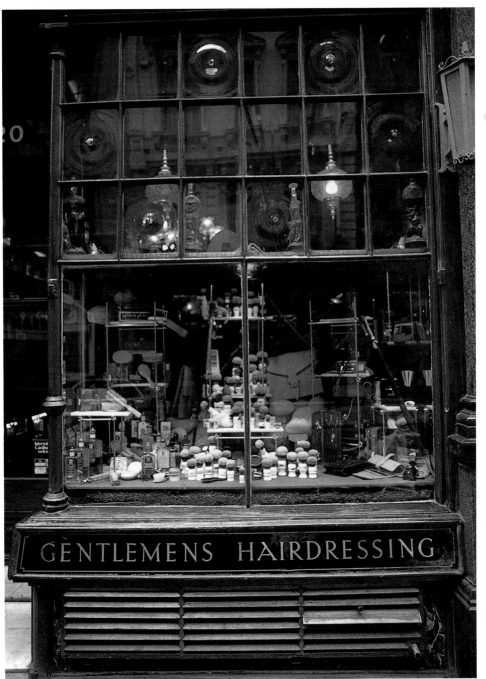

GENTLEMENS HAIRDRESSING

Left *London's shops range from the antique to the modern, the general to the particular, the conventional to the weird, and the humble to the extraordinarily grand. Some, like this smart barber's establishment, have preserved their pre-1914 fittings and atmosphere, creating in the passer-by a momentary feeling of being carried back to the London of gas-light and Sherlock Holmes.*

Left *The capital's most celebrated hatters, Lock's, have been at the same premises in St James's Street since 1764. Lock's made the plumed hat worn by the Duke of Wellington at Waterloo in 1815 and created the first bowler hat in 1850.*

Left *The uniformed beadles of the Burlington Arcade are stationed there to make sure that the rules against running, singing and carrying an open umbrella in this august Regency shopping precinct are not transgressed. The arcade with its small shops has been altered several times since it was built between 1815 and 1819.*

Above *The wine department of Fortnum and Mason. This smart Piccadilly grocery was opened in 1707 by William Fortnum, an ex-footman to Queen Anne. It became well-known for supplying ready-made hampers to the aristocracy and for sending traditional English delicacies to console exiles in the remotest corners of the British Empire.*

Left *Pringle's of Scotland, a knitwear manufacturer, proudly displays the royal warrant in Savile Row. The street has been famous for the last hundred years for its fashionable men's tailors.*

London

Right *The Soho area, a warren of narrow streets and alleys to the west of Charing Cross Road, is known for restaurants and strip joints, and for a Continental atmosphere which extends to foreign provision shops. This one in Old Compton Street still delivers by bicycle.*

Below *Theatrical costumiers and fancy dress houses add a histrionic strand to London's shopping fabric. The Theatre-Zoo in Earlham Street, off Cambridge Circus, specializes in animal masks, costumes and make-up.*

Below *Provisions on a more sumptuous scale in Harrods, the queen of London shops and possibly the most famous shop in the world. It began as a humble village grocery in Knightsbridge in the 19th century. The mouth-watering Art Nouveau food halls date from the early 1900s.*

Following spread *Hung with 11,000 light bulbs and haughtily domed, Harrods sears the night sky. Not only can you buy anything from a piano to a parrot inside, but Harrods will bank your money, insure you, kennel your dog and finally bury you. The great store was founded in 1849 by Henry Charles Harrod.*

London

Left *Markets are another lively feature of London life. These trolleys are in the Covent Garden area. The city's principal fruit, vegetable and flower market was moved away across the river to Nine Elms in 1974 and the site has been transformed into an attractive piazza of shops and cafes – reverting to its fashionable character of the 17th century.*

Left *A stall in the Sunday morning street market in Petticoat Lane, near Aldgate. Officially Middlesex Street, it earned its popular name from its old clothes dealers.*

35

♛ ♛ ♛ ♛

Opposite page *Stalls and shops selling antiques and bric-a-brac have been a dominant feature of the Portobello Road market, on Saturdays, since World War II.*

London

Right *The old Covent Garden market area has become a focus for perky shops, boutiques and open-air entertainments. It was originally the walled garden of the Westminster Abbey monks. In the 1630s Inigo Jones turned it into an Italian-style city square, which soon attracted a street market.*

Below *Bright and shiny, fruit and vegetables are the main items on offer every weekday in Soho's cramped, cheerful Berwick Street market. There has been a pub on the Blue Posts' site since 1739 or earlier.*

37

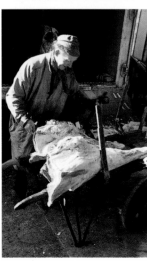

Left *Live cattle were sold at Smithfield Market until halfway through the 19th century, driven in lowing herds through the streets to the market and away again. This was stopped in 1855 and a new dead meat market was built, whose future is distinctly uncertain.*

London

Below *An eye to the main chance at Sotheby's in Bond Street, where millions of pounds change hands at art auctions every year. One of London's two leading auctioneers, Sotheby's was founded in 1744 and four successive generations of the Sotheby family ran the firm until 1861. It moved to Bond Street in 1917.*

Right *Galleries and auction houses make London one of the capitals of the art world. This bulky modern sculpture stands in the Serpentine Gallery in Hyde Park, in a building where ladies and gentlemen delicately sipped tea in Edwardian times.*

Left *The rival auctioneering firm of Christie's was founded by James Christie in 1766. A friend of Reynolds and Gainsborough, he built up a flourishing and fashionable business in art sales. His son, also James, moved the firm to King Street in St James's in 1823 and it has been there ever since.*

Opposite page *The stately classical portico of the Tate Gallery, opened in 1897, belies the aggressively modernistic objects inside, for besides British painting the Tate also houses the national collection of modern painting and sculpture. The gallery was named after Sir Henry Tate, the Tate & Lyle sugar magnate, who paid for the building.*

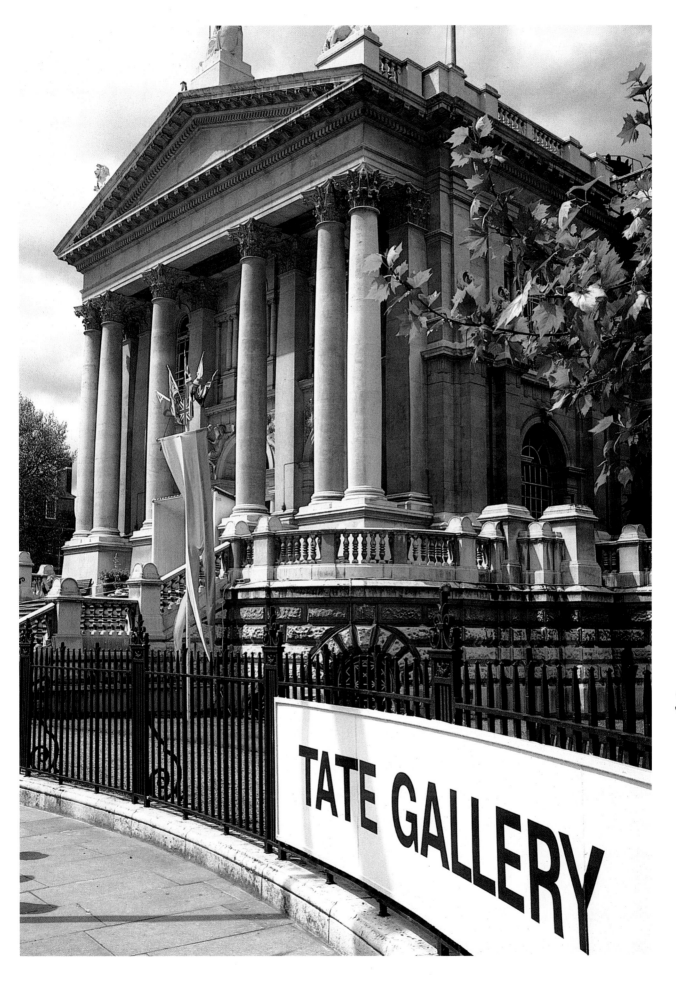

London

Above *The shades of evening gather round the floodlit 'Mother of Parliaments', in Westminster beside the Thames. The building is on a heroic scale. The river frontage is 940ft (286m) long and the square Victoria Tower, at this end, rises to 336ft (102m). The tower of Big Ben at the far end is 320ft (97m) high and the minute hands of the great clock are 14ft (4m) long.*

Left *The building dates from the 1840s. Designed in mock Gothic by Sir Charles Barry and A W Pugin, with 1000 rooms, 100 staircases and two miles of corridors, it replaced the old Palace of Westminster, which burned down in 1834. Inside, a main central corridor links the House of Lords, at the nearer end, to the House of Commons, closer to Big Ben's clock tower.*

Below *Maritime history,
navigation and astronomy
blend at Greenwich, where the
Observatory was built in the
1670s on the orders of
Charles II.*

Left *The brass rod marks the line of the Greenwich Meridian, internationally accepted as the line from which degrees of longitude, east and west, are measured.*

Left *The figurehead of the Cutty Sark, which breasted the waves to China as the fastest tea-clipper of her day. Launched in 1869, the magnificent sailing ship is now preserved in dry dock at Greenwich.*

43

Left *Greenwich Palace on the bank of the Thames downstream from the heart of London was a popular residence of the Tudor and Stuart monarchs. It was rebuilt in the late 17th and early 18th centuries to Wren's designs as a hospital for crippled seamen of the Royal Navy, and is now the Royal Naval College. In the background is the old Queen's House, built for James I's queen by Inigo Jones.*

London

Below *The shining morning face of London's Dockland, where derelict docks and run-down housing are being replaced by expensive office and residential blocks in the latest architectural mode. Up to World War II, London was the country's biggest port, but in the 1960s a rapid decline set in.*

A & B KINGHEN

Above *Opened in 1987, the new Docklands Light Railway links Dockland with the City as an artificial artery channelling life back into a decayed area. Automatic and driverless, it connects the Isle of Dogs with a terminal near the Tower of London.*

Left *The old face of Dockland: a worn-out crane in front of a grimy warehouse in Wapping. London's original importance was as a port, from Roman times on, and for many centuries the Thames was the main highway between England and the Continent.*

Above *Buses in the London Transport Museum, Covent Garden, which tells the story of the transportation system in a city whose surface traffic now moves no faster than it did a century ago. The horse-drawn omnibus contrasts with the familiar red double-decker motorbus in the background, an instantly recognisable symbol of London anywhere in the world.*

Left *From rocking horses to model forts by way of dolls, teddy bears and toy theatres, exhibits illustrate the ephemeral and yet eternal world of childhood in Pollock's Toy Museum, in Scala Street, off Tottenham Court Road. Benjamin Pollock, who had a shop in Hoxton in the 1930s, was one of the last makers of toy theatres.*

47
♛ ♛ ♛ ♛ ♛

Opposite page, below *The great gateway of the Natural History Museum in South Kensington, a beautiful mammoth of a Victorian building by Alfred Waterhouse. Beyond this imposing portal, dinosaur skeletons, the Whale Hall and the stuffed African elephant vie for attention with birds and butterflies, corals and fossils, and the story of human evolution.*

Above *The planes in the Royal Air Force Museum at Hendon range from the Bleriots and Sopwiths of the first heady days of flying to the Hurricanes, Spitfires and Lancasters of World War II, and on to more recent types. The collections survey RAF history from all angles.*

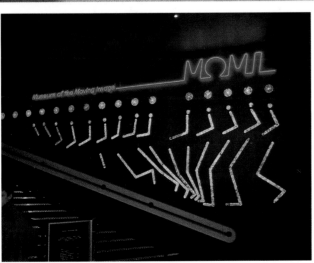

Left *A suitable sign for one of the capital's newest and most enjoyable attractions. The Museum of the Moving Image, opened in 1988 on the South Bank, applies the latest 'hands-on' technology to the starry history of films and television. Charlie Chaplin, Marilyn Monroe, all the great and glamorous names are on parade.*

Right *The grounds of Hampton court, on just as palatial a scale as the house, were laid out in formal style in the time of William III with trees and long walks, a fountain garden, orangeries and a wilderness area with a maze.*

Left *Cardinal Wolsey built Hampton Court with its sumptuous gatehouse in red brick. A monument to his wealth and success, it had 500 rooms, more than half of which were for guests. Henry VIII appropriated it before the cardinal fell from power in 1529 and made it bigger still. He built the bridge leading to the gatehouse, guarded today by the heraldic King's Beasts.*

Left *The sunken garden at Hampton Court. Generations of monarchs loved and cherished the palace. Henry VIII, Elizabeth I, Charles II and William and Mary all added to the beauties of the palace and its grounds, and William IV and Queen Victoria later repaired and restored them.*

Left *The legal profession has created enclaves of peace in the heart of the capital, on the same model as Oxford and Cambridge colleges. The inns of court were originally hostels for lawyers and students, and now provide the 'chambers', or offices, of legal firms. Lincoln's Inn, with its attractive gardens, has been on its present Chancery Lane site since at least the 1420s, and probably earlier.*

Left *Over the doorway the golden griffin on a field of black is the badge of Gray's Inn, founded in 1357. Shakespeare's* Comedy of Errors *was first performed in the hall of Gray's Inn, which was reconstructed after being bombed flat in 1941.*

53

Left *Staple Inn in Holborn was one of the inns of Chancery, where Chancery Court clerks were housed and trained in the 14th century. It was later taken over by nearby Gray's Inn to house aspiring students, and is now used as offices.*

Right *Looking across the Thames at night to the Royal Festival Hall, part of the South Bank arts complex. Planned by the London County Council's architects, the concert hall is the only building left from the 1951 Festival of Britain. The river front was faced in Portland stone in the 1960s.*

Left *The stars wheel in their courses on the hour every hour at the London Planetarium and there are special laser shows as well. Opened in 1958, the Planetarium is half of a double bill with Madame Tussaud's, the famous waxworks next door. The original Madame Tussaud came to England from France in 1802, bringing with her casts of the heads of victims of the guillotine: some can still be seen in the Chamber of Horrors.*

55

Left *The London Hippodrome, designed by the great Edwardian theatre architect Frank Matcham, opened in 1900 as a combination of circus and music hall. Between the wars musical comedy stars like Jack Buchanan and Cicely Courtneidge graced the boards here. The Hippodrome later became a restaurant and night club.*

Following spread *Tulips and tourists on duty outside Buckingham Palace. The Queen's 600-room London residence, originally the town house of the Dukes of Buckingham, was bought for the royal family in 1762 by George III. George IV and the architect John Nash made it palatial. In front is the white marble monument to Queen Victoria, crowned by a gilded figure of Victory.*

Far left *London is a city of statues and monuments, of which the most famous is Nelson's Column in Trafalgar Square. The 17ft (5m) statue of the great naval hero was hoisted to the top of its granite column in 1843.*

Centre left *The Monument in Fish Street Hill in the City is 202ft (61m) tall and stands 202ft (61m) from the spot in Pudding Lane where the Great Fire of London began in 1666. Built in 1671–77, it was designed by Sir Christopher Wren and Robert Hooke, and there is a fine view from the top.*

Left *The winged griffin near the foot of Chancery Lane marks the western boundary of the City of London.*

59
♛ ♛ ♛ ♛

Above *The grand old Duke of York (1763–1827) atop his column in Waterloo Place. He was Commander-in-Chief of the Army and a day's pay was docked from every serving soldier to pay for his monument.*

Left *Cleopatra's Needle, close to 70ft (21m) tall on the Embankment, was brought to London from Egypt in 1878. Items buried under it include a Bradshaw's railway timetable and a dozen photos of the prettiest Englishwomen of the time.*

Below *London is especially rich in monuments of the self-confident Victorian Age, presided over by the Albert Memorial in Kensington Gardens. The seated statue of the Prince Consort, 14ft (4m) high, is sheltered by a Gothic canopy, and surrounded by elaborate groups of statuary. Designed by Sir George Gilbert Scott, the monument was completed in 1872.*

60

Right *'Turn again Whittington . . .' The monument to Dick Whittington and his cat is near the foot of Highgate Hill, on the spot at which the future Lord Mayor is said to have heard Bow bells telling him to return to the city where he was to make his fortune.*

Above *One of London's most popular landmarks, Alfred Gilbert's statue of* Eros *dominates Piccadilly Circus, where it was unveiled in 1893. The fountain commemorates a generous philanthropist and social reformer, the seventh Earl of Shaftesbury. The circus itself dates from 1819, when John Nash's new Regent Street crossed Piccadilly on its way north. It is now considered the hub of the West End.*

Index

The page numbers in this index refer to the captions and not necessarily to the pictures accompanying them.

Acknowledgements

All the photographs in this publication are from The Automobile Association's photo library, with contributions from:

M Adelman, S & O Mathews, Barrie Smith, M Trelawny and T Woodcock with the exception of:

Front cover: Spectrum Colour Library – Horse Guards Parade; Tony Wiles – Tower Bridge.